ALTAN
TiMPA
GOES TO THE SEA

Europa
editions

Europa Editions
116 East 16th Street
New York, N.Y. 10003
www.europaeditions.com
info@europaeditions.com

Translation by Michael Reynolds
Original Title: *Pimpa e il mare*
Translation copyright 2007 by Europa Editions

Library of Congress Cataloging in Publication Data is available
ISBN-13: 978-1-933372-32-7

Altan
Timpa Goes to the Sea

Book design by Emanuele Ragnisco & Federico Francucci
www.mekkanografici.com

Printed in Italy
Arti Grafiche La Moderna – Rome

CONTENTS

TIMPA AND THE PUPPYFISH

AND YOU KNOW HOW TO DO IT?

YES.

THEN IT CAN'T BE THAT DIFFICULT.

IT'S NOT THAT EASY EITHER, YOU KNOW?

CAN YOU SHOW ME HOW IT'S DONE?

NOT RIGHT NOW...

...BUT I CAN SHOW YOU A PICTURE.

OH, YES!

IT'S FROM A FEW YEARS AGO.

THAT'S FOR SURE. YOU'RE THIN.

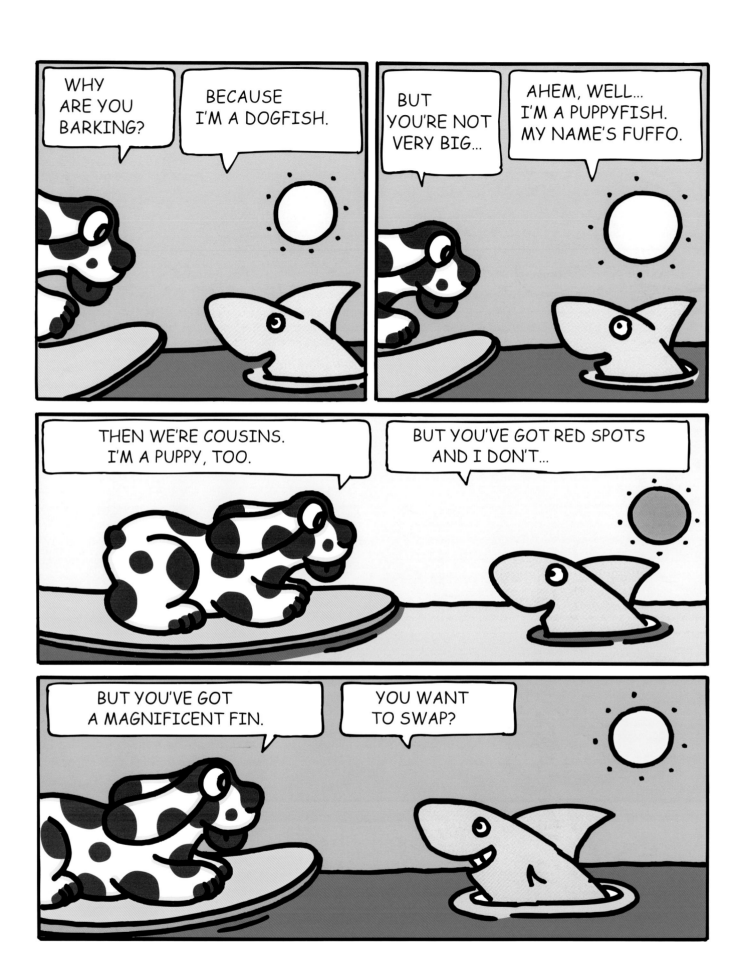

TIMPA AND SPOTTY ARMANDO

TIMPA AND THE UNDERWATER SLIDE

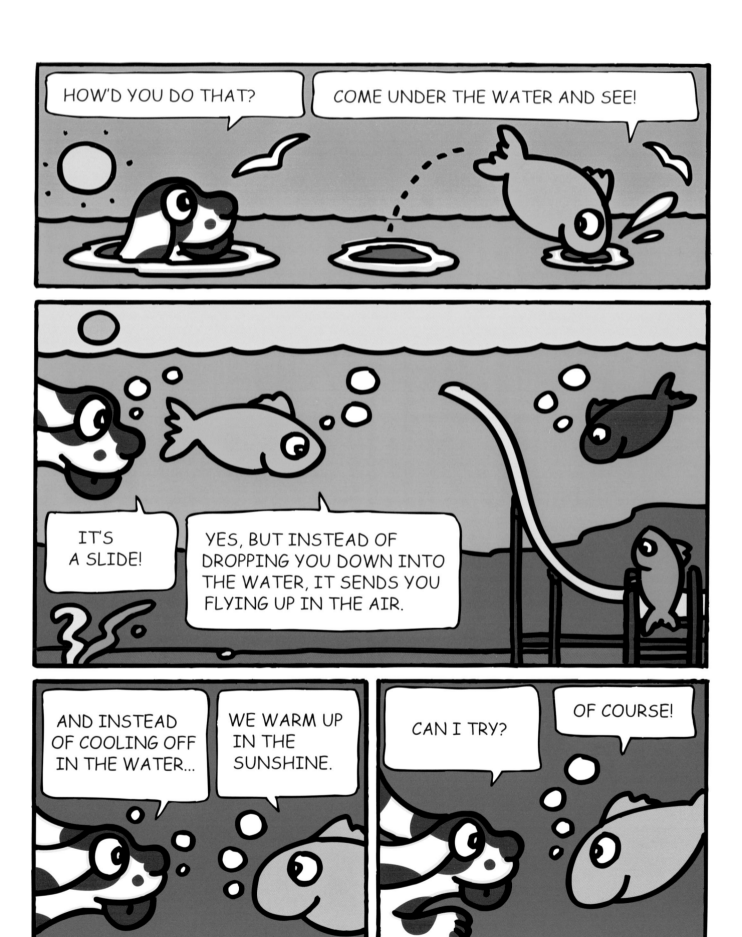

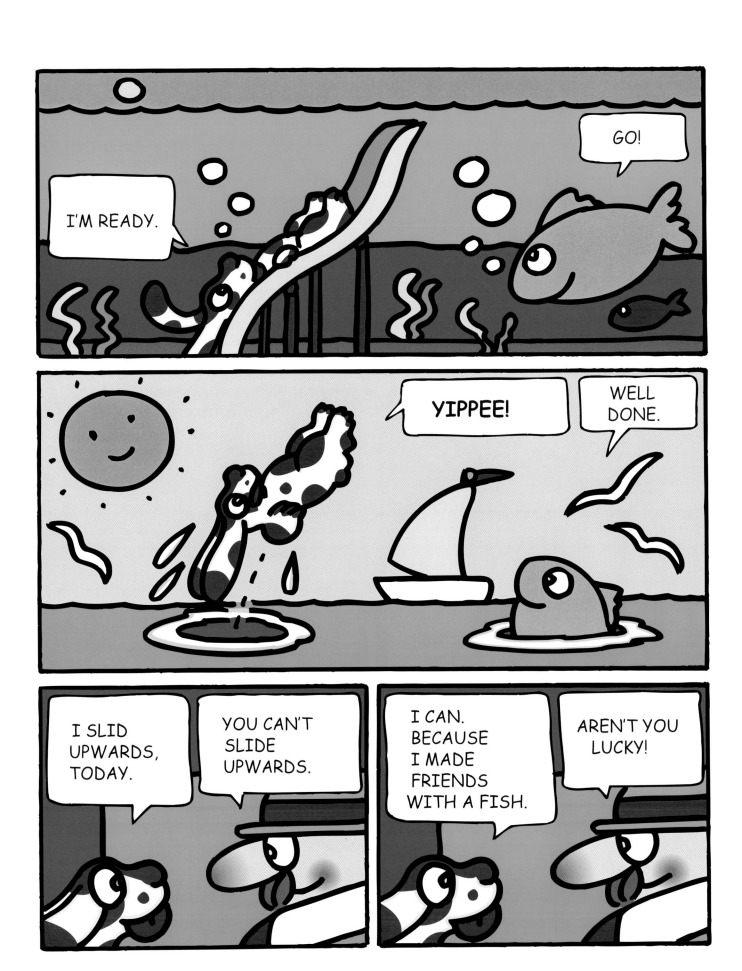

22

TIMPA AND THE DOUBLE-SCOOP, SAND-FLAVORED ICE CREAM CONE

ICE CREAM REALLY IS A DELICIOUS THING.

YEP.

IT'S A SHAME IT DOESN'T LAST LONGER.

YEP.

IDEA! WANT TO PLAY A TRICK ON ARMANDO?

YES.

TIMPA AND THE PEARL

TIMPA AND THE DOGFISH

TIMPA AND THE DIVING SUIT

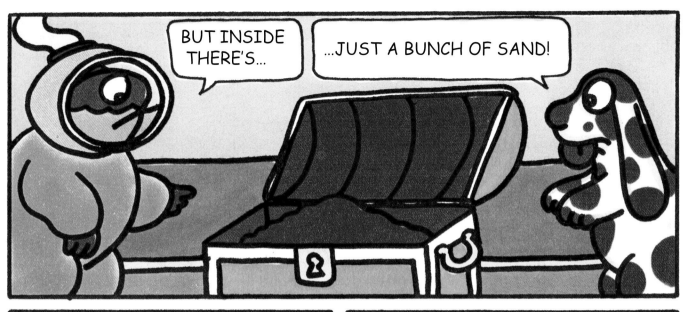

38

TIMPA AND TITO WHO TURNS RED

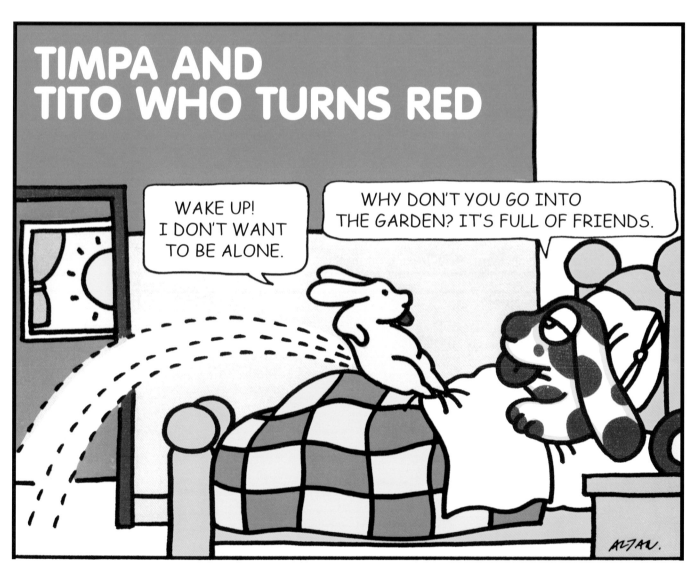

41

TIMPA AND THE FLYING FISH

The Big Question
Wolf Erlbruch
52 pp • $14.95 • 13-digit ISBN: 978-1-933372-03-7

Winner of the Ragazzi Award at the 2004 Children's Book Fair in Bologna.

A stunningly beautiful and poetic illustrated book for children that poses the biggest of all big questions: why am I here? A chorus of voices offers us some answers. But nothing is certain, except that as we grow each one of us will pose the question differently and hear different answers.

The Butterfly Workshop
Wolf Erlbruch (illustrator) and Gioconda Belli
48 pp • $14.95 • 13-digit ISBN: 978-1-933372-12-9

"A magnificent book! This clever tale is a kaleidoscope of nature, full of rich language and practical advice for making dreams come true."—Judy Rothman Rofé, "Madeline"

For children and adults alike . . . Odair, one of the Designers of All Things and grandson of the esteemed inventor of the rainbow, has been banished to the insect laboratory as punishment for his overactive imagination. But he still dreams of one day creating a cross between a bird and a flower. A story about the power of imagination and the importance of following one's dreams.

The Miracle of the Bears
Wolf Erlbruch
32 pp • $14.95 • 13-digit ISBN: 978-1-933372-21-1

"Children who already know (or think they know) how to answer bear's query will be rolling in the aisles."—*Kirkus Reviews*

A children's tale about the beginnings of life. One spring, waking from a long winter sleep, a young bear finds himself longing for a family of his own. But how to get one? He asks advice from an array of animal friends, but none of them really seems to know. Then he meets a female bear and things look as if they may be heading in the right direction. Erlbruch's moving illustrations animate this tasteful story with all the colors of plentiful springtime.

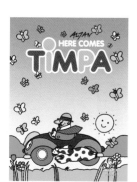

Here Comes Timpa
Altan
48 pp • $14.95 • 13-digit ISBN: 978-1-933372-28-0

"A veritable classic that every home must have on its bookshelves," said the influential Italian newspaper *La Stampa* about Altan's irresistible character, Timpa. "She is a friend to wile away the hours with. […] She observes the world with interest, deep feeling, respect and wonder." Timpa has been the best-loved children's character in Italy for decades. In this first book of the Timpa series, the kind-hearted Signor Armando and the fun-loving Timpa make each other's acquaintance while out picking strawberries. Altan's marvelously colored illustrations and the charming dialogues are bound to capture children's hearts.